Are You The One?

CLORETTA D CHANDLER

Scripture quotations noted NKJV are from The Nelson Study Bible, copyright © 1997 by Thomas Nelson, Inc. Used by permission.

"Scripture taken from the AMPLIFIED BIBLE, Old Testament copyright © 1965, 1987 by the Zondervan Corporation. The Amplified New Testament Copyright © 1958, 1987 by The Lockman Foundation. Used by permission.

Are You The One? Copyright © 2015 Cloretta D. Chandler

ISBN-13: 978-0692384671

Published by Cloretta Chandler Ministries, LLC
Lithia Springs, GA

All rights reserved. No portion of this publication may be reproduced, stored in a retrieval system or transmitted in any form by any means – electronic, mechanical, photocopying, recording, or any other except for brief quotations in printed reviews without prior written permission of the author.

DEDICATION

This is dedicated to those who honor the institution and privilege of marriage.

CONTENTS

Acknowledgments

Preface	Pg 1
Introduction	Pg 3
Love Story 1 - Chan & Rose: Marriage Made In Heaven	Pg 4
Love Story 2 – Sean & Joan: Happily-Ever-After	Pg 7
Love Story 3 – John & Jane: Restoration	Pg 13
Love Story 4 – Elwin & Madison: Marriage Bliss (I Think?)	Pg 23
Love Story 5 – Nadine & Warren: Till Death Do We Part	Pg 29
Words of Wisdom	Pg 40
My Discovery	Pg 43
About the Author	Pg 45

ACKNOWLEDGMENTS

First all honor and glory to God for the courage to bring an idea to life. Thank you for your guidance

This endeavor would not have been possible without the cooperation, inspiration and assistance of my family and friends.

To my family: my parents Pastor F.L. & Rosetta Chandler the pillars of the Chandler Legacy; to my siblings David, Loretta, James & Kelly and to "my children" my nieces Kayla & Lauren and my nephews J.C. and Jonathan thanks for loving me like you do.

To Angela Feliz for not thinking it robbery to take time out of your very busy days to assist a co-worker and a friend and edit this little book.

And finally a very special thanks to my friends:

Mr. & Mrs. Webb
Married for over 40 years. They were the first couple to say yes in sharing their love and life. What a romance.

Mr. & Mrs. Carter
Married for over 30 years. What an awesome testimony to our God as a God of a second chance.

Mr. & Mrs. Backer
Married for 6 years. They seemed to be enjoying every minute of it.

Mr. & Mrs. Donovan
Married over 35 years. Living, loving, overcoming and savoring every moment of their marriage.

Thank you for sharing your inimitable love stories and marriages. You have allowed me and all reading this book access into your worlds as husbands and wives, lovers and friends and showed us how
God has joined this man and this woman.

The names have been changed to protect the identity and privacy of these couples and their families.

PREFACE

Ever since my first crush on my childhood sweet heart I knew I wanted to be a wife, a mother and a home maker. And if I had anything to say about it, all of this was to begin when I turned 19. At least that was my plan. But if you are a believer, well if you are human, you know things don't always go the way we plan. I am now in my mid 40's, a minister of the Gospel of Jesus Christ and a college grad and yes I am also STILL SINGLE; never been married and no kids.

Please know it's not because I haven't tried, because I've tried. A lot. I've been engaged three time and I have a gorgeous wedding dress hanging in my closet from the last engagement. Soooo…I've tried. However, as difficult as it has been at times with being a brides maid and not the bride; being the God-Mother and not a mother myself and then watching my friends get EVERYTHING I've been praying for and wondering "God is it EVER going to happen for me?" AND NOW, my biological clock is running down and about to STOP! Most days all I can say is "Really? REALLY?!?" But nevertheless I have chosen to hold on to the hope that one day… (Lord one day sooner than any later, pleeeeeaaaaasssseeee) but one day I will find and be found by Mr. Right and have that huge wonderful wedding and live a wonderful married life. Cause after waiting this long you can BELIEVE it's going to be WONDERFUL!!

Now some of you reading this may be saying to yourself 'Oh, that's so sad, you're a childless old maid.' while others may be saying "Girl you don't know how truly blessed you are not to have that head-ache". In either case I still have a burning desire to be that wife, that mother and that homemaker. Now don't get me wrong, I have a great life and I'm very grateful for who I am and whose I am. But I just believe – no, I know that I know that I know, God has a "he" just for me.

So in my waiting I thought, hey, why not do some research and see what it takes to make a good marriage a great marriage. But not through books that talk about marriages and how to make a marriage work, keep a marriage exciting and strong, but by interviewing those who are in it, living it. So I did and this is the result.

Oh, as a United States citizen I think it's important to point out, especially in the wake of marriage no longer being defined as a legal union between one man and one woman, that this composition is focused on heterosexual relationships. I believe in Holy Matrimony between a man and a woman. And being a heterosexual kind of gal and a believer that God intended and still intends for marriage to be between one man and one woman...well you know.

With that said I hope you enjoy the love stories you are about to experience and come away with renewed hope and faith in marriage and in love. I know I did.

Enjoy!

INTRODUCTION

Times they are a changing: *"We The People"* just re-elected our first Black, oops I mean first African American President and for the first time in our nation's history we have universal health care known as the Affordable Health Care Act to some Obama Care to others and (although I am not a supporter) we also have marriage equality. In the midst of all these changes and advancements one thing has remained the same my marital status - SINGLE!

As a slightly over 40 not hard on the eyes single woman I often wonder if my Mr. Right is still waiting for me and if so will I recognize him when he comes. With couples divorcing, the definition of "marriage" changing and those that "stick it out" seem so unhappy, how can I be sure that the same won't happen to me? Is there a formula to prevent prolonged unhappiness in a marriage? Is there a guarantee that my marriage will not end in divorce court?

I don't know about you but at times I'm just terrified that I'll end up with "Mr. Wrong" because of desperation or alone because I never found my "Mr. Right". Or I won't recognize the "Love of My Life" when he's staring me in the face. All I know is I don't want to miss him when he comes.

So, what to do, what to do? Then it came to me, why not talk to married couples and ask them how they were able to recognize their mates. So I did and I have to say after talking with these couples I found out that…well before I tell you what I found out about locating **"The One"** why don't you have a look at what these couples had to say, then I'll share with you my discovery.

LOVE STORY 1: MATCH MADE IN HEAVEN CHAN & ROSE

One of the greatest love stories every told is that of my parents Chan and Rose. My parents have been married for over 51 years. Amazing in this day and age. But what's more amazing is they raised four great and awesome adults (if I do say so and I do). During their marriage they were the spiritual leaders of a thriving church for over 40 years; they built a youth center and mentored other pastors and church leaders. They did all of this after only knowing each other for 2 weeks prior to their wedding. Yes, you heard me correctly. TWO WEEKS. Here's how the story goes...

Dad:

After returning to the States from a four year tour in France I transferred to the Air Force Academy in Colorado Springs, Colorado. John F. Kennedy just won the presidency and gas was 25 cents a gallon and I was an associate minister at St. John Baptist Church. While in the pastor's study, a lovely young lady on the Cover of the Kansas City call newspaper caught my eye. I read the article and saw that her brother was the Pastor at new Hope in Kansas City, Missouri. I told my Pastor I was going to drive six hundred miles and find her to propose and return with her as my bride. There were other ministers in the office at the time and they all laughed at me. But I was determined. I knew that she was the one. I wrote her a letter to introduce myself and asked if I could come see her. She wrote me back and said. Yes.

When I got there, her family was very protective. Her mom did not like me at all. I just wanted to take her out, but Rose was busy. She said, if I wanted to see her, I would have to go with her to her rehearsals and church. She had a lot of them, but she had a beautiful voice and I loved her, so I went to every single one and I finally got my date. We went to a drive-in movie. I don't remember the show, but I remember Rose and wanted to start my life with her right away.

I went to her home to ask her father for her hand in marriage. He told me, "My Rose is grown. We have already raised her. Don't put your hands on her." I knew exactly what that meant and promised to love and protect her. But Rose's mom did not care. She said her baby was too young and she would not let me marry her. No way.

Mom:
When I met Chan I was ready to get married. I thought he was cute in his uniform and the more we talked the more I knew I wanted to marry him too.

At that time my siblings and I had a singing group The Porter Four. So for the week that Chan was in town I took him to all of our practices and singing engagements. He was a trooper because we were everywhere. Later that week he asked me to marry him. My father gave me permission to marry Chan, but my mother did not like him at all. She said he was too slick. I had to basically sneak off and marry Chan. We made arrangements to be married on his way back from visiting his parents in Mississippi and then move to Colorado.

My sisters helped me get a wedding dress together and we were married by the minister, right after church service. I wanted to start my life right away with Chan, but had to wait. He had to get back to Colorado, so I followed later on the train. But we wrote letters to each other to keep in touch and soon he picked me up at the station and we started our lives together.

Ok, ok wait. Mom you barely knew Dad. No, I stand corrected, you didn't know dad beyond his first and last name. You hadn't met his parents, his siblings, or anyone else who knew him. Why would you marry a man you just met?

Mom:
Like I said, I was ready to get married and I liked the way he looked in his uniform. (lol).

Dad:
> It's not that farfetched Coco. When God is directing your steps He will always lead you in the right direction and to the right person at the right time. Just stay in tune with the Lord.

Thanks mom, thanks dad for the reminder that trusting in the Lord is the best way to go. Proverbs 3:5-6 says it best "Trust in the Lord with all thine heart; and lean not unto thine own understanding. In all thy ways acknowledge him, and he shall direct thy paths" (NKJV).

LOVE STORY 2: HAPPILY-EVER-AFTER
SEAN & JOAN

Our next couple has just celebrated their 40th wedding anniversary and the best way for me to characterize their marriage is to say they are a living example of a Prince Charming and His Princess with a major emphasis on *Happily-Ever-After*. While talking with Mr. & Mrs. Webb (Sean and Joan) whom I affectionately refer to as "Daddy Sean and Momma Joan" it was very evident that each of them put the needs, wants, and happiness of the other before their own. As a result of witnessing such admiration the first thing I wanted to know and ask on your behalf was…

At what point did you know your spouse was the person you wanted to spend the rest of your life with?

Joan:
>He was different from any boy I had ever met. I guess we had the same mind set. We could talk about everything. We were on the same wavelength. It just seemed right. Like this is what it is supposed to be. I could talk to him about serious issues and he would understand.

Sean:
>I had decided after high school I was going to go into the service, make a career of it then get married. Then, my sister introduced me to Joan. I believe the Lord spoke to me and said now! One night, while Joan and I were sitting in the car talking; I told her, if you weren't still in school I'd marry you and she said "I'd marry you anyway." I just knew she was the

one. I didn't see anyone any better. When the Lord gives you something He always gives you the best.

Daddy Sean that is so true. God only gives the best. Heavenly Father all I can say is that when my Mr. Right meets me he doesn't see anyone any better either.

Why did the two of you want to get married?

Sean:
After we met, I knew there was nobody else. Everyone in my family wanted me to marry someone else but God said to marry Joan. No regrets, never looked back after 40 years. The marriage has grown stronger. That's what the Lord wanted for me. I'm glad I did what God wanted me to do.

Joan:
Time for a change. I felt like I had met the person I wanted to marry. I was 18 years old when [we] got married. No regrets. Sean is the best thing that has happened to me. I can't imagine being married to anyone else. We've had disagreements but we always worked it out. I've always been able to count on Sean. A lot of women can't count on their husbands, I can. He is my "Knight in Shining Armor". I can say that because there's never been anything I came up against he was not there for me. When my health began to go down, Sean told me to rest and not to worry about how we were going to pay bills just rest.

Did you seek guidance from God as to whether or not your spouse was the one for you and you for them?

Sean:
I honestly can't say I prayed about it but I know God was directing it. I had so many opportunities to go the way of the world. But, I just couldn't do it. I've been in situations that were dangerous but God had His hands on me. Throughout the crazy things I did and wanted to do God has always watched over me. I would not be here if it had not been for the hand of God. I don't know. I just knew the Lord instilled in me this is what I want for you regardless of what anyone else has to say. This is it. I knew Joan

before I knew her. We were both down to earth. God has blessed us.

Did you have any counseling on what it was going to take to have a successful marriage and what to expect and not to expect?

Sean:
Not with a professional, we talked to three people, Uncle Frank, Uncle Potts and Reverend Lay. They just told me to always let home and wife come first before mother, brother, sister and father. And if you're ever off somewhere and you meet some female and she asks if your married don't ever deny you're married.

Joan:
Uncle Frank also said never to let your wife carry things that are too heavy and whatever is outside that needs to come into the house Sean should do it.

What were your expectations of the marriage and of your spouse? Were those expectations met?

Joan:
Sean has fulfilled my expectations. I wanted someone who would stay beside me throughout the good times and the bad. I can't honestly think of any major complaints, little things yes, but no life altering things.

Sean:
Yes! I really didn't know what to expect until I moved out. Everything I expected fell into place. She was my expectation and she met my expectations and more...the things I didn't know she knew and what she didn't know I knew. We sort of grew together.

Did you and Mr. Webb wait until the two of you were married before you had sex for the first time?

Joan:
I was 18 years old, but, I felt like this was something that God meant for us to do; to come to each other pure. You don't start out a marriage without making that commitment. When you give yourself to somebody that's all you've got.

It's a precious gift God gave us and He doesn't mean for us to give it to everybody. And somewhere along the line I had just made up my mind not to do it. Sean asked me if I thought people should have sex before they got married and I said no.

Sean:
I really wanted to but after that night God said don't go that way anymore. If we had I would have believed the stories, that Joan was a "kept" woman by married men and I would not have married her.

How important is sex in a marriage in your opinion?

Sean:
VERY IMPORTANT! Just as important to me today as it was when we first got married. I thank God that I still have the same feelings for Joan, stronger now than before. I thank God that I still desire my wife. I'm grateful for what God has given us. I feel sorry for people who no longer feel the same about their spouses.

Joan:
I agree, it is important in a marriage. It's all the things that your life means. It's the coming together. For instance you bake a cake, a layered cake but it's not a cake until you put the icing on it. That's what sex is to a marriage.

Are there or have there been any disappointments in your marriage? If so, how did you deal with them?

Joan:
A disappointment is something you either wanted to happen or didn't want to happen and it continues; defining it that way I'd have to say no. As you grow older you learn more and I'm glad I've grown.

Sean:
No, I have never been one who wanted a whole lot, just fine cars maybe (giggle) and Joan was sort of like that, whatever I got she was okay with it.

What factor or factors have contributed to the longevity of your marriage?

Sean:
> Patience, love and the willingness to share even when you don't want to. You have to be willing to share how you feel about things.

Joan:
> And compromise, lots of compromise.

Did you hear what they said about one another *"He is my Knight in Shining Armor"* and *"I didn't see anyone any better"* WOW!! What a testimony. Daddy Sean and Momma Joan are definitely living 1st Corinthians 13.

There was so much more they shared with me that I wish I could share it all with you, but if I did there wouldn't be room for the other couples I talked to. So let me suffice to say that in the Webb marriage their love for one another is strong and their marriage is living proof that...

- Love suffers long – *"I wanted someone who would stay by me"*

- Love is kind - *"just rest Joan"*

- Love does not envy - *"I knew there was nobody else"*

- Love bears all things - *"when my health began to go down...Sean was there"*

There is one more thing I'd like to share with you before we move on to our next couple, something Momma Joan said that bears repeating, she pointed out that "you can't decide for anyone who they should marry, that's between them and God." Think about it.

In Loving Memory

Mrs. Francis Joan Webb was called home to glory on November 2, 2007. Just one month before she and her "Knight" were to celebrate 46 years of Holy Matrimony. As Momma Joan's health continued to decline Daddy Sean never left her side, fulfilling her heart's desire that she would have "someone who would stay by me". Only in death did they part.

Momma Joan we love you and miss you. Until we meet again…

LOVE STORY 3: RESTORATION
JOHN & JANE

John & Jane Carter could fill a book all by themselves with a legendary tale of love, heartache, forgiveness and restoration. If ever someone needed proof that God is indeed a healer and a deliverer, John & Jane's saga can most defiantly testify to that fact.

John & Jane are faithful members of their church and in the community. John is a Police Detective and Jane is a Civil Servant. Although they do not have children of their own they are and have been parents to many. Their work in the community as mentors has helped to change lives and point young women and men in a new and better direction.

We begin our discussion with Jane. This is Jane's second marriage after a failed first. But I'll let her fill you in on the details. I will say this, Jane is living proof that God's grace is sufficient, listen…

Jane what is different about your current marriage as opposed to your previous marriage? Why is this marriage working when the other did not?

Jane:
> I was immature in the first marriage. I was 19 and right from my parent's home. I had very strict parents, but I wanted to live on my own and live the life of a wife. I fantasized that I would always be happy and always in love. Years passed and I realized it was not all happiness and it wasn't all love.

Even though I knew of God I did not have the relationship with God that I have now. I was raised in a Christian home and taught that a wife takes care of her husband regardless of how she feels. I wasn't allowed to be myself; I got lost.

After the marriage broke down I learned I had to depend on me only. I had no balance in my life. I went from one extreme to the other extreme. After the marriage broke down I told the Lord I would never do this again. But after being single for a while I knew that my ministry was to be married. I wasn't really happy single.

In this marriage I went in knowing that there would be problems and I wanted to marry my friend. I learned that a friendship is very important to a marriage. In my previous marriage I learned what worked and didn't work. With this marriage I tried not to bring baggage into the marriage. I got some good advice not to punish John for what my ex-husband did. I was very honest with John. I told John no matter what don't lie to me, even though at times John was a little to frank.

Jane, what was the cause of the break-up of your first marriage? Why didn't it work?

Jane:

Low self-esteem on my part and adultery on his as well as no communication. I felt like we had to feel love and be together all the time. As years went by he didn't want to be with me all the time only when he wanted to go "clubbing".

When I learned of his infidelity it was a painful time. I found out about his infidelity and other things through the grape vine. One of my sister-in-laws had to bring it to my attention and she didn't like me anyway. Not once did I involve God as I think back. But I know he never left me.

When I would go to church there was this lady who would sit in the back and as my sister-in-law described the woman my ex-husband seeing I knew who she was.

When I first found out about her I felt like a failure, because I felt like I didn't do all that I could have done. After a while I came to a point where I was willing to share him. I was being sarcastic but if she was going to share the fun she could share the work.

Then I started to lose me because of the pain of feeling like a failure. I started drinking because I didn't want to feel anything. The pain started out as a constant head ache. My doctor told me I was on the verge of a break down. I cried every day for a year because I wasn't dealing with the problem because I didn't want to admit I was unhappy. So I covered it up with pain pills, alcohol and slept all the time. I didn't feel anything. I didn't care. I wanted to die but at the same time I didn't want to die. I just wanted to make the pain stop. So I took an over dose of pills. But my ex-husband and his sister found me and made me throw them up. I had even left a suicide note with funeral plans. My mom, well she was actually my grandmother, but she raised me – she saw the note and confronted me and asked what was so terrible in my life that I wanted to die. And I could not tell her. So I kept it all in because she liked my ex. So she asked me, do you know what that would do to this family?

I decided to talk to my natural mom and she understood what I was going through because she went through the same things. "Don't make it easy for him by dying" she said. "How long do you think he would mourn you?"

So I started to live in all the wrong ways. Everything I said I would not do I did. After all this started we stayed together 6 more years. I started feeling really angry toward him. He would accuse me of being with other men. I wasn't but after a while I did. If I had it to do all over again I would not have done it.

After a while as time went on I found out that my ex was into witchcraft more specifically roots. But God still watched out for me.

He [the ex-] didn't like anybody that liked me or wanted to support me. He just wanted me to stay close to him and his family only. He especially didn't like my friend Bernice. "She's changing you" he would say. So my ex-husband told me not to eat anything except what he gives me. A bell went off in my spirit not to eat anything he gave me.

One day while I was in the bed wide awake mind you, I heard a voice tell me "If you stay here you will die." So to make a long story short I left. I told him I was leaving. He didn't believe me. So when I went home I asked a friend to help me move. He said he didn't want to get involved but my other friend let me use his truck. - - I set my new apartment in order and sat and waited to feel regret, but I felt good and I felt it was right.

I left in May, got a promotion on my job in June. Everything started going right. My ex- tried to beg me to come back. He even tried to bribe me back. We were separated for a year when I asked him for a divorce. I was happy. I got my lawyer and she said to take him to the cleaners but I didn't want to do that I just wanted my freedom.

On the day of the divorce when the judge said you are free to marry if you so choose, I cried. I cried because I felt like a failure. Not long after that I bought a house and everything fell into place. God had His hand on me the whole time.

After a while I started to grow very bitter toward men. They weren't good for anything except to service me and to be used. My supervisor noticed something was very wrong. I told him what was wrong and he told me I needed to lower my standards. All I wanted was what I didn't have in my first marriage. Someone to love me take care of me defend me and let me be free to love him. One night I cried out to God to send me a man. I didn't want to be alone and God sent John. At first I didn't want anything with him but a friendship. But God had other plans.

For seven days in Florida while on vacation we spent every day together. By the seventh day I started to give in to my feelings for him. But I would still fight it. I would always put conditions on our relationship. After he asked me to marry him I said I would only if my mom, the woman who raised me, approves and if she approves then we'd have to be engaged for a year. He said, "piece of cake". Two months into the engagement he called and said "Jane, how would you like to get married in California?" which meant my family couldn't make the wedding so all my friends got together and made sure I had everything I needed. We were married at twelve midnight in August.

Why at Midnight?

Jane:
Because I wanted something totally different, so I flew out to California.

John:
With 27 pieces of luggage.

Jane:
We were married in Reno Nevada. The wedding started on August 9th and ended on August 10th. The first six months of our marriage while stationed in Hawaii for three years was a total culture shock for me.

John:
It was the first time Jane had been away from her family and her first time out of Georgia for longer than seven days.

Jane:
I was whining and depressed. John told me to get myself together. I didn't want to work, nothing. But as time passed we began to bond because we were all we had.

John at what point did you know Jane was the one you wanted to spend the rest of your life with?

John:
When I first met her, because I had mentioned I had been praying for a good wife.

How did the two of you meet?

John:
>My friends Nancy & Rufus took me to the post to meet some nice ladies. One Friday night when we were out at the post I walked around the club looking at all the young ladies. When I went back to the table where Nancy and Rufus were sitting Nancy asked me what was wrong. I said nothing; the woman I was looking for wouldn't be here until tomorrow. The next night I looked around and told Nancy that's her sitting over there. I'm going to ask her to dance, afterwards I'm going to talk to her and after we talk for a while she's gonna like me. After she gets to know me she's gonna fall in love with me. After she falls in love with me, she's gonna marry me. Nancy and Rufus laughed and I walked away.

Jane:
>He came over asked me to dance and after we danced we talked for quite a while and he didn't hit on me. So I decided he was either married or he was gay. So I asked him,
>>"Are you married?" he said
>>"no". Then I asked him,
>>"then you must be gay" he said
>>"why gay?" I said
>>"because if you don't have anybody and you're not in love with somebody you must be gay."
>
>But we continued talking and of course he wasn't gay and I really enjoyed talking to him.

What made Jane stand out?

John:
>I just felt Jane was the one. I prayed for her.

And Jane the same question.

Jane:
>His attitude and the way he carried himself and the night we met he hadn't hit on me all night.

John:
>One of the things I liked about Jane she was the first lady I met that I had an interest in where we just sat and had a conversation about what we do and what we believe and sex never came up. Most of the ladies I'd talk to before that would tell me or lead me to believe within an hour or two of our conversation that I could sleep with them. So I enjoyed the conversation with no strings attached.

Did the two of you wait until you were married before you had sex for the first time?

John & Jane:
>No!

Why Not?

Jane:
>At first all I wanted was a child but no husband.

John:
>The attraction of Jane being single and having a job – she had it going on (giggles).

Since neither of you waited until you were married to have sex, did either of you feel guilty?

John:
>I think Jane did.

Jane:
>Yeah, but I think I was still trying to fill a void.

John:
>No, I didn't feel guilty. I was enjoying my favorite sin.

Now that you are married in your opinion how important is sex in a marriage?

Jane:
>Very important but not the foundation. It is a benefit. You have to build on more than sex. Cause once the sex

is gone it's not too much more to stand on if sex is the foundation. Things happen; illness. You have to have a solid foundation.

John:
When we first got married on a scale of 1 to 10 I weighed it at a 9.75. It was pretty important to me. It's still important but when we first got married sex was the closeness between us. Now…because we've been through family issues and tragedies we have drawn closer together…

Jane why did you want to get married again, especially after the "drama" you went through in the first marriage?

Jane:
Because I didn't feel whole as a single person; even though the first relationship turned out bad the institution of marriage was still good. I never lost that.

John this is your first marriage correct?

John:
Yes.

Why did you want to get married?

John:
Well, I was tired of being single, lonely; tired of playing games with crazy women and I thought I'd have sex anytime I got ready.

John, did you always want to be married?

John:
I had given myself a goal. I would marry by the time I was 30 – until then I would sow all my wild oats. All that changed at age 26 when I met a woman who seemingly was the answer to my prayers. She changed my standards.

Jane:
And I did something I thought I'd never do, marry a younger man. I assumed he was older than me. He

carried himself as an older person. He's 3 years younger than me. It wasn't until we were serious did I ask him how old he was. God set me up! (lol)

How long have the two of you been married?

Jane:
Seventeen years.

What factor or factors have contributed to the longevity of your marriage?

Jane:
Prayer, forgiveness and friendship.

John:
Prayer, forgiveness, loving heart, patience, restoration with God as individuals.

Did you have any counseling on what it was going to take to have a successful marriage and what to expect and not to expect?

John & Jane:
No.

Jane what would you have liked to have known about John before you got married that you learned or found out after you were married? Would it have changed your decision about marrying him?

Jane:
If I had known about John being younger than me I would not have married him, but God concealed that fact. It never occurred to me to ask that question. I just assumed he was older. Another thing I said was I never wanted a bald headed man.

John:
But I wasn't bald headed at the time. - - [to answer your question] the myths Jane was taught about sex and the skeletons she brought into the marriage.

John & Jane, the two of you have had to confront infidelity in your marriage, would you mind sharing how in the world the two of you were able to make it through, especially you Jane, since you had been through it before with your first husband. What kept the two of you together? Even to the point where you both can talk about it and share the experience with others with no ill feelings or animosity or residue?

John & Jane: <u>GOD!!!!</u>

I told you their saga was a good one. I'm happy to report that John & Jane are still growing in love and in strength. In 2005 Jane was diagnosed with breast cancer. With chemo and radiation treatment she lost a lot of weight and all of her hair. But GOD!!! I am very happy to report that Jane Carter is not just a survivor but an overcomer. She is healthy, happy and cancer free. Her husband stood by her side and prayed her through. Today she is vivacious and blessed. To God be the glory.

LOVE STORY 4: MARRIAGE BLISS (I THINK?)
ELWIN & MADISON

If there were ever two joyfully married full-grown kids, Elwin and Madison Backer are them. They laugh together, cry together, console one another and they thoroughly enjoy one another's company and most of all they are absolutely "crazy-in-love" with one another.

Elwin and Madison have been married for five "honey-moon" filled years going on six. And they act as though they just "fell-in-love" yesterday. Elwin is an associate pastor and Madison is a devoted "first-lady-in-waiting". They have two beautiful children, a lovely young teenager and a somewhat shy adolescent.

This is Madison's second marriage and Elwin's first. They have had some challenges in their young marriage but they are happy go lucky and seem to be doing quite well. It's apparent these two are crazy about one another. As Elwin drools over Madison like he could *"slop her up with a biscuit"* and Madison gawks at Elwin as if he is the finest specimen of a man she has ever seen or will ever see; it was time to begin the interview. I started out by asking...

Elwin & Madison how long did the two of you date before you got married?

Elwin & Madison:
Not long [we dated] for a year and a half.

Madison:
Well actually it was about one year and nine months; if you count the three month grace period we tried to be

friends.

Elwin:
> On the third day after we met we started dressing alike. It was on a Thursday night during revival. The first night we met Madison was wearing peach. I'll never forget that!

Madison why did you want to get married?

Madison:
> Because I'm a family oriented person and I wanted companionship.

And why did you marry Elwin?

Madison:
> Because he was (and is) a God fearing man.

Elwin same question, why did you want to get married and why did you choose Madison?

Elwin:
> I've always wanted to have a wife and have a family. I wanted someone to share my life with, someone to wake up to in the morning and to go to be with at night. I chose Madison because I believe now as I did then that Madison was given to me by God. Through early trials that tested our love for one another, we still remained together (which) confirmed that God truly did give me Madison. Listening to the voice of God I asked her hand in marriage.

What kind of trials?

Elwin:
> Simple misunderstanding such as a ready-made family. There was some adjustment in that because of her experience in already having and raising two children [from her previous marriage] she had a step-up on me, but because of my belief on how children should be raised was on occasion conflicting. Another conflicting issue for me was constantly being late because of Madison's procrastination. That was a big conflict. I had always been a person who strived on being on time, but we were

always late because I didn't want to go ahead of Madison, I wanted us to arrive together.

Elwin, how did you know it was love and not lust?

Elwin:
>One reason I knew, going back to the conflicts I spoke about earlier, when conflicts came out that tested our relationship to the point where the average couple may say I don't have to put up with this, like a ready-made family and procrastination, I felt something strong that helped me to stay with Madison. If everything in our relationship was peaches & cream I would not have had anything to base our love on.

Madison how did you know it was love and not lust?

Madison:
>The anxiousness to be in his presence and he had a warm spirit. It was just a flow. We fit. To be in his company was like a broken puzzle that had been completed.

Elwin:
>She was ravenous for me. ☺

Mrs. Backer, Madison, this being your second marriage, how does Elwin differ from your first husband?

Madison:
>Elwin lived and practiced the Christian life. He's constantly remembering that he is a Christian and I'm a Christian. Just like James 1:22-23 "But be doers of the word, and not hearers only, deceiving your own selves. For if any be a hearer of the word, and not a doer, he is like unto a man beholding his natural face in a glass"(NKJV). He is a doer of the word and not a hearer only. His lifestyle manifested these words.

At what point did you know Elwin was the one you wanted to spend the rest of your life with?

Madison:

After spending quality time and not to his knowledge interviewing him.

What type of interview?

Madison:
I'd ask him questions like, after we have our last child what method of birth control would we use? Because I feel it would be unfair to place the entire burden on me to be the one to go through surgery or to take birth control pills. We discussed budgeting, finance and love making creativity.

Did the two of you wait until you were married before you had sex?

Elwin & Madison:
No!!! The temptation; couldn't wait; couldn't hold out!

Did either of you feel any guilt?

Elwin & Madison:
Yes, big time.

So was it just once?

Elwin:
Oh, Lord no!!!

Madison:
There were times when we did practice abstinence, but we fell again.

Since the two of you couldn't wait was the sexual ability of your soon to be spouse a major factor in whether or not you would marry them?

Elwin:
No, it was not a factor. I believe that I could not control my flesh in that area. I still knew that God had given me Madison.

Madison:
No, because I could have waited until we were married.

In your opinion, how important is sex in a marital relationship? What if your spouse lost their ability to engage in sexual intercourse?

Madison:
> If he lost his ability, it would take some adjusting, however, God being God He will make a way out of no way. I wouldn't leave him.

Elwin:
> I think that it is important in a marital relationship because it, it keeps that intimacy between spouses. However, if Madison lost her ability to perform, I'd still remember my commitment I made to God and to her; 'For better or for worse'.

So you really meant that commitment?

Elwin:
> Yes! That's why people don't stay together now.

The two of you have been married for five years now, if you could go back and change anything, do somethings differently, what would it be? What would you change?

Madison:
> I would have married my husband sooner and would not have had sex before we were married.

Elwin:
> I would have changed us not having sex before marriage and I also would have married Madison sooner. And I would have wanted us to take a class on the roles of a husband and the roles of a wife. Marriage 101: What to expect and what not to expect.

How different was the transition from living single to living as a couple?

Elwin:
> I've always had the ability to adapt so it wasn't difficult. The desire to be together was so strong that adapting was easy.

Madison:
    No it wasn't hard.

Elwin, this being Madison's second marriage and your first was there any baggage from Madison's first marriage? If so how did you deal with it?

Elwin:
    I believe by her being married before and having two children before we got married, there were challenges from the start. However Madison somehow tended to have made me feel more wanted and accepted into her life, comfortable.

Elwin and Madison it looks like the two of you are headed in the right direction. With God in the mix you're sure to be together "until death do ye part".

I'm very sad to report the Backers did not survive the storms that life threw into their marriage. Mr. and Mrs. Backer have divorced and gone their separate ways. I don't know all the particulars to why this marriage failed, however, I can say that through it all they each leaned on God for support to endure the pain and to give and receive forgiveness as they went their separate ways. Elwin and Madison have begun new lives with new spouses and where they are now they are happy.

LOVE STORY 5: TILL DEATH DO WE PART
NADINE & WARREN

At the time of this interview our last couple was one month away from celebrating their 36th wedding anniversary when tragedy struck. Mr. Warren Donovan suffered a massive heart attack and died at home with his best friend, his lover, his wife, his life at his side Mrs. Nadine Donovan.

Although Warren wasn't present in body he was most defiantly present in spirit and in love. As Nadine and I sat talking and reminiscing about the days and years gone by I began this interview by asking...

At what point did you know that Warren was the one you wanted to share your life with?

Nadine:
>Warren and I had actually known each other all our lives. Our parents knew each other, we went to high school together and when we were young we use to play together and I would come home telling my mother "Warren always bites me" and my mother would tell me to bite him back (giggle).
>
>When we were in high school he was the last person, the very last person I thought I would like because he was too vain. Every time he passed by a mirror he was looking at himself. I'd tell him "you are not that cute".
>
>He would always tell people "you loved me then and you love me now". Truth was no I didn't. It wasn't until after he enrolled in the service and we both left home (childhood home in Colorado) that we

actually started corresponding. I was comfortable with him, very comfortable with writing to him. When he would come home I was comfortable being with him. I felt safe. I said to myself I could be married to him and I wouldn't have a problem.

We had come home to (Colorado) to visit and I can't remember what we were doing and I looked at him and I was like *WOW!* Okay I could be with him for the rest of my life because I was comfortable with him. He made me feel like I was somebody. I always felt like I was just this little church girl; sheltered and he made me feel like I was the most beautiful woman in the world. He would look at me as if it was just me and I was like WOW! So I said I guess I'd keep the old boy. (laughter)

Why did you want to get married?

Nadine:

Because I was getting old. (laughter) Seriously! I was 22, girl I was getting old! That really is the reason why I wanted to get married because I was getting older.

Ok, ok, I just have to say to my readers you can imagine, I'm feeling really ancient right about now in this interview but I digress...please continue...

Nadine:

I was 22 years old and back then if you were getting close to 25 you were pushing it – you know you were supposed to be married by then. And I felt this was my one and only chance so go for it. (laughter) So I did.

Did you seek God's guidance as to whether or not Warren was the one for you and you for him?

Nadine:

Yes, but before I prayed I recalled a 5th Sunday program where one of the missionaries spoke on what to look for in a husband. She also said there are some things that you as a Christian woman look for that a non-Christian wouldn't look for and that number one thing is his love for God as well as how he lived his life. Was God number one in his life and if you were to come into his life would he lead the household as a Godly man or just as a man? And I saw that in Warren. I saw how dedicated he was to the Lord and I saw how dedicated he was to his church. So I watched him as he went about living his life. He didn't raise what I called a ruckus he was very low key.

So yes I prayed. I remember saying I wanted a man that loved Him first and loved me and he would be a very good father to our children by leading them in the way that they should go as far as the Lord was concerned. And I found that with Warren. The love he had for God was just amazing to me. I was very happy. I just watched him and said *WOW!*, you're alright!

What were your expectations of the marriage and of Warren? Were those expectations met?

Nadine:
My expectations were that he would have God as the head of our household. That it would be God first, then him, then me. I expected him to treat me with respect and I would do the same for him. I expected him to lead our household as the head of our household. I expected him not to walk ahead of me but that we would walk side by side. When we first married it was kind of shaky because we were both new at it. We didn't have a courtship so we weren't seeing each other on a regular basis.

So you and Warren really didn't date?

Nadine:
No, we didn't. We did all our corresponding through the mail. He came home to visit and then the next time he came home we got engaged and the next time he came home we got married. So we didn't really have an "I go to your house, you come to my house, you pick me up and we'll go out on a date". We didn't have that we did all of our "dating" through the mail.

Was this while he was in the service?

Nadine:
Yes.

Oh WOW!!

Nadine:
Really, because when I tell people that they are like "and you married him?" YEAH I DID!, because I truly believed that Warren was going

to be my husband. I would even say to family and friends "When Warren and I get married...this and that" so much that my brother would try to correct me by saying "he hasn't even asked you yet" my response to that would be "he will". I was just that confident in knowing that Warren was going to ask me to marry him. I felt we were right for each other.

Did you wait until you were married before you and Warren had sex for the first time?

Nadine:
    No, no. We were rowdy.

So it was in-between those visits when he came back home?

Nadine:
    Yeah, yeah...but no we didn't wait and afterwards we both looked at each other and said we're not supposed to do this but we did so now what are we going to do? Warren said "well I'm going to be gone" I said "that's a good answer"(laughter).

Did you and Warren feel guilty?

Nadine:
    Very much so. But the reason I did it was because I wanted to be sure that I was going to satisfy him. Because I had grown up in church and I didn't know anything.

Sheltered?

Nadine:
    Very, very sheltered. When I was young my mother would tell me if you kiss a boy that means you're pregnant so the first time I kissed somebody I worried for days.

Oh my gosh!

Nadine:
    Because I was sheltered I didn't even know that you were supposed to enjoy sex. I was brought up thinking that sex was a part of a wife's duty. But then I found out (smiley face) and went bucket wild! (lol)

So, you found out you could enjoy this...

Nadine:
> HEY!!!

...so with that said, how important is sex in a marriage?

Nadine:
> I believe people put too much importance on sex because they don't realize that there will come a time -- anytime during a marriage -- when sex becomes the last thing on the list. Due to sickness, due to just not wanting to, to it's just not fun anymore.
>
> When you first marry yes, that's the one thing you want to do all the time. It's like you can't get enough of it and then as you progress on in your marriage you find out that it's not - it's not an every night thing. You may do it maybe you know once or twice a week. Maybe one's feeling it and the other is not.
>
> It's important when you first marry because that's what you base your relationship off of for a lot of people. There are people that marry and don't have sex at all and that could be because there is [something wrong physically]. People look at sex as sexual intercourse, the penis entering the vagina, and that's [all] they look at...There are so many different ways to have sex without having sexual intercourse and [many] people don't know that.
>
> A young couple [that just got married] don't understand that there is more to it. Because as you get older he may not be able to get an erection anymore due to him being sick. Or she may not lubricate like she use to due to illness. So you find other ways to satisfy each other.
>
> It used to be when Warren would barely touch me my body would just *"DING! DING! DING! DING! DING! We are getting ready to do something wake up, wake up we are getting ready to do something"* and then he'd turn back over and go to sleep and I'm like "WHAT?", were you dreaming or what? I'd get up hostile the next morning [and he wouldn't know what was wrong].
>
> Sex is more than the penetration. Sometimes just holding each other you're still having sex. Just rubbing each other's skin you're having sex. Because if you are so in tune to your spouse the slightest thing can make you just have an orgasm and you haven't even had intercourse. I

could hear his voice and it would feel like somebody is just pouring syrup all over me and that's just hearing his voice. I loved to hear his voice. That's what I miss most about him now hearing him call my name...it was a nice turn on. Just melt. (huge smile)

Where there any disappointments in your marriage and how did you handle them?

Nadine:
> At first the disappointments where something that I couldn't discuss with him because we weren't on that level yet where we would talk to each other. We would hold all that in...I finally sat him down and said we need to talk. And he would say "oh, here we go". But we did we needed to talk because you can't get through a marriage without talking to each other.
>
> For example Warren made a decision without talking to me he bought a car. [He] didn't say 'Nadine I'm thinking about buying a car' [or] 'you know I'm looking at this car'. [Instead] I came home and saw this little car out front and I'm thinking okay he's using one of his friend's cars but it never went away.

This was early on in the marriage?

Nadine:
> Yes, this was early on in our marriage and I said ---
> > "Well whose car is that? he said
> > "Mine."
> > "Okay, hum how long have you had it?"
> > "A while."
> > "Okay, soooo..."
>
> Automatically I was hurt because he didn't discuss that with me and I told him that hurt.
> > "It hurt that you felt like you couldn't discuss purchasing another car with me when my funds are helping to pay for it".
>
> He said,
> > "Well no, it's coming out of my money"
>
> I said
> > "No it's not your money and it's not my money it's our money. It's all going in the bank in the same account. It's our money."
>
> I was very disappointed so I talked to him about it.

We were young and when you're young you make stupid mistakes you don't think about how it will affect the other person. Did it get better, eventually it started getting better because he started realizing that what I do affects her. And what I do affects him and so we learned to communicate.

Did you find that as the two of you started to communicate more that he didn't always understand where you were coming from and vice versa?

Nadine:
Yes.

How did you work through that?

Nadine:
I made it a point not to wear my feelings on my sleeve as they say because he would do something or say something and I would get offended. I just felt like he didn't trust me enough and vise verse.

The trust issue is very hard, especially if a mistake has been made once and it was a devastating mistake to where you get so far down that now you are trying to climb your way back up and it seems like you keep going farther and farther down because I'm trusting you that when I go to work and I get paid and the money goes in the bank that you are going to do what needs to be done and that is take care of our bills and then I find out that you are not doing that, that trust issue is gone.

So you have a choice to make. You can [either] take that control away and do it yourself or you sit down and come up with a plan. I took it away. You have a problem with money. You have a problem with paying things and paying them on time. And it wasn't so much that he had a problem he just wasn't [that] concerned. [For example] it's due on the 15th I'll go in on the morning of the 15th and pay for it. You got the money at the beginning of the month and it's due on the 15th you don't wait until the 15th because you know how you do with money you start pinching (spending a littler here, a little there) so by the time the 15th comes you don't have enough; so you can't do that. So that happened and he always called me tight, you so tight you make a dollar scream. Yes I will! But I'll have some money! (lol)

I'm a very low key type of person to where if I have my rent paid all my utilities paid gas in my car and I have food in my cabinets I'm fine. I don't need anything else. I will make a meal out of what I have. I don't have to go out to eat. It bothered him more to see me come home from working all day and then start "working" at home cooking dinner. Hey, it's a part of life. It didn't bother me, but it bothered him because he didn't want to see me doing that because he worked at home and I didn't. So when I would get home every evening he would have my bath water ran, dinner started and by the time I got out of the tub dinner was done. It was hard for me to get use to that but that bath sure did feel good after a long day.

How did you know it was love and not lust or just infatuation?

Nadine:
When I looked at him one day after we had been married for 10 to 12 years. I was in the kitchen cooking and I turned around and looked at him. He was laying on the couch just snoring to beat the band as always and I just looked at him. I looked at him real good and it's just like this feeling came over me that I never felt before and I was like wow I love this man. I really love this man. He was everything, he was my knight in shining armor. I knew that if I got sick that he would take care of me. I knew that if I was hurt that he would be there. I knew that if I needed to be comforted that he would put his arms around me and hold me and tell me it would be okay.

When he died all of that went away and God took over. It's like you pass a baton to the next runner and they pick it up and run the race. And I believe that's what happened when he died. He passed me to the Lord to take care of me and the Lord has been my comfort. I have always found my strength in Warren. I would come home and I would just go off and he was my sounding board and he never said anything. He would just sit there and listen. He was my strength. I looked at him that day and that was everything that I saw. This was a strong man and I was so lucky to have him in my life to have him as my husband I was so proud of him and of what he was doing. He could be so tender and he could be so rough at the same time and I loved him with everything that was in me. And it was like wow he belongs to me he's mine. That's my husband and I loved him and I still love him. I will always love Warren Solomon Donovan.

Should the Lord send someone else in my life Warren will always be my first love. Nobody can replace him. I say right now if I were to go into a relationship I would be comparing that person to him so that's not something I want to do soon anyway. But I'm not saying I'm not lonely. I liked the companionship. We talked we laughed and not having somebody here to laugh with (starting to cry) that's what make it hard at times but for the most part I still talk to him in my heart. I still laugh with him in my heart. And I love him. When you hear a person say 'I love you so much it hurts' that's the way it was with us.

The love that we had we never said it out loud to each other we weren't the type [to banter] 'I love you' back and forth. We would go out to dinner and I would sit there and pour my heart out to him and he'd look at me and I really think he's into what I'm saying and then he stop and say "y'ah man".(tears turn to laughter) Come on now. So I got use to that. And he would tell me 'Do you know how much I love you?' And I would tease him and said 'no, tell me' he'd respond 'I love you, you know I love you don't you?' and I'd say 'Are you trying to make me okay with it or what? Are you trying to convince me about this or yourself?' But I knew he loved me. I knew because he showed his love to me and that was the best thing. I guess we were okay you know. We survived each other and it worked.(smiles)

When you first got married did you discuss having kids or was it let's see what happens?

Nadine:
When we first got married how he proposed to me was he said "Would you marry me and be the mother of my children?" And before I said yes I said "how many children are we talking about?" I said I need to know because I've got to prepare all of this for what we are about to do here. And he said six. I said "SIX?" I took a deep breath and said okay, the Lord is good he's able. I said how 'bout we start out with three. After we do thee then we'll see about doing the other three. Well we had Sol and we didn't go no further.

Now I will say that I had three miscarriages and Sol was the only child that we had and after that I said you know we still got some more to go, we have 5 more to go are you ready? He's response was "well we'll see what the Lord has in store for us".

We did discuss it but my body however didn't do what it was supposed to. I think because I wanted a child so bad that my body fought against me a lot. And when I got pregnant with Sol I had prayed and asked God to please bless me. If I only have one child I'll be okay. I wanted more children but if I had the one I would be okay and that's what happened and I got a humdinger.(lol)

What factors contributed to the longevity of your marriage for 35 years?

Nadine:

I say number one we talked. We let each other know what our expectations were going into our marriage. We asked those questions are you happy? Are you satisfied?

You asked those questions throughout the marriage?

Nadine:

Yes. We would try to fix those things we were lacking on. There comes a point when you are married that somebody has to get off the marry-go-round, stop the *'I'm not speaking to you'* games. Somebody has to be willing to give in - him or her - and point out that we are not together. We are on opposite ends. You have your own opinions and each person should allow the other person to have their own opinions. It can't be I like this, this, this, and this and that's the way it's going to be that's the way our house is going to be set up because I like it. Forget about what you like. It's not about you it's about me. You can't have that.

Marriage is a give and take. You have to be willing to forgive and that's very hard to do. To say I'm sorry. To say I'm sorry I hurt your feelings. Or to tell your spouse you hurt my feelings by what you said or by what you did. I don't appreciate you doing or saying that. Letting your spouse know how you feel about whatever it is makes for a better marriage. If you hold it in you start talking to other people about he doesn't do this, he doesn't do that and so on and so on.

It's also important to discuss your sex life, your likes and dislikes. Either you or your spouse or both were sexually active before the two of you got married and you or he starts doing something the other has never experienced before and he or she is put in a position they are not comfortable with. You have to be willing to say I'm not comfortable doing that and that person has to understand if you're not comfortable but it's something you want as a part of your relationship you have to discuss it.

Those factors that come into play you have to be able to sit that person down and talk to them. Your spouse should be your best friend. You should be able to tell them anything. I don't like this and say why. Each one should bring their own opinions to the table and talk until you work something out.

Get a plan together. If it's a budget or we are going to have sex three days a week instead of four; I think we should buy a blue car verses red. My point is you have to discuss. People don't discuss. They want it their way or the high way. You can't do that and have a successful marriage.

When Warren and I were on the marry-go-round I got off and told him what wasn't working for me and then he got off and we sat down and started talking. Different things started popping up and we talked about them all night. We went to sleep and work up continued the conversation and finally started understanding each other. To the point where I could be thinking about something like dinner and I'd mention to him what I was considering for dinner and he would say "we've been married to long" I'd ask why you say that because that's exactly what I was thinking. But that comes from talking and finding out about each other - talking to each other verses talking at each other. Communication is a very big factor in a marriage.

Nadine thank you so much for sharing your love affair with Warren and how the two you made your marriage a happy and safe place to love, learn, play and grow. You and Warren are an inspiration to me. Thanks for sharing.

WORDS OF WISDOM

What advice do each of you have for singles today who hope to marry for the first time or again?

Sean & Jane:

Jane:
>Don't' rush. Don't leave anything un-discussed, because one may want children and the other does not. Discuss everything that will affect your marriage.

Sean:
>Seek God's guidance and He will let you know if this person is the right one for you.

John & Jane:

John:
>My advice is to both the single man and the single woman; first and foremost if there is anything you could not forgive him/her for don't marry her/him. Learn to be friends before you get involved because if it wasn't for the friendship Jane and I developed, we would probably be divorced by now.

Jane:
>Have a relationship a real relationship [with God], not just when you need Him.

John:
>But not just with Him (God) but with her too. When your potential wife tells you things and warns you of things especially of other women, listen to her and understand she can see some things we men

don't see. Example Jane can see when another woman is interested in me, she can see the ulterior motives before the man ever picks up on it.

Jane:
First for the women, know yourself your weaknesses and strengths. Be secure in yourself. Have a relationship with God make Him your man first. And if a man doesn't treat you like God treats you then don't waste your time. He can't change himself and you can't either. That's not your job. For the men, just don't expect her to be a 'sex pot'. If you really want to have a really good sex life, get in her head. That's the main sensual sex organ a woman's brain.

Elwin & Madison:

Elwin:
To the single man that wants to marry my advice is to make sure that his relationship with God is in order. And when that woman comes into his life listen to the voice of God more than your own desires and wait. I believe that in seeking God he will also lead you to the God fearing woman who is also seeking God and has the same desires.

Madison:
My advice to the single woman is to make sure he is a God fearing Christian. When somebody is a God fearing Christian everything else will fall into place.

Nadine

Nadine:
I would tell a single woman if you are looking for a husband be specific in what you want. Don't be afraid to ask God for what you want because He will give you just what you ask for. Why not tell God what you want. I told God I want a man that loves you first. A man that will put you above all others. A man that will treat me with loving kindness and that will treat me like I should be treated. I want a man that is going to be a good father to my child. That will instruct my child in the way he/she should go. That's the kind of man that I'm looking for.

You don't go and say I want him tall, dark and handsome. Begin with character because that's what's going to have a lasting relationship. You find out now that people if they've been married for 10 years that's a stretch.

You don't have to try out the merchandise before you buy it. Why buy the cow [when] you [can] get the milk free. That's a true statement. Let it be a surprise on your wedding night. Let him open that package for the first time.

If you have been doing that and now you're looking for a husband stop all that. Present to whomever the Lord brings into your life a clean vessel. You have had sex and been out there just running amuck; but when you stop and decide I want to live my life for Jesus then stop all that... When you go to your husband it's almost like coming to him as a virgin again. When you get yourself cleaned up God will do the rest.

MY DISCOVERY

After spending time with these couples and documenting their journeys it has been confirmed for me that marriage is not an "I'll never feel lonely again" remedy or "I'll have sex whenever I want it" strategy. No, marriage is WORK and takes WORK, lots of WORK. However, the good news is that marriage will work out quite well if both the husband and the wife talk things through and work it together.

I've also learned that marriage – especially a Christian marriage - is also a ministry. A ministry of two distinct individuals becoming one unique being - "and they shall become one" (Genesis 2:24b, NKJV). In this ministry with a huge congregation of two the goal is to serve one another, cherish one another, care for one another and fulfill the emotional, physical and mental needs of one another.

Marriage is not all about what one spouse can get out of it from the other spouse just to please and satisfy self. No, rather it's about what each "fearfully and wonderfully made" (Psalms 139:14, NKJV) counter partner has to offer to create a more perfect and unique union. These men and women became something greater together than they were alone. They became ONE.

> "And the Lord God took the man and put him in the Garden of Eden to tend and guard and keep it…Now the Lord God said, It is not good (sufficient, satisfactory) that man should be alone; I will make him a (suitable, adapted, complementary) helper meet for him" (Genesis 2:15;18, Amplified Bible).

God made for Adam a woman that would complement him and balance him – his equivalent. Both made in the image of God to fulfill the will of God and one another

Each of these couples knew in their hearts and in their spirits that marriage was for them. That one day they were to be husbands and wives and they pursued it. How did they pursue it you may ask? Well I can tell you it was not in the clubs, even if that is where they met. And it was not in the church, even if that is where they met - but in their prayers. Now you may be saying to yourself right now, hold on there not all of them prayed before they decided to marry their spouse. You're right. Well you would be right if prayer was only about people talking to God. Prayer isn't just us talking to God it's also about God talking to us provided you have an ear to hear what the Spirit of the Lord is saying.

So what have I discovered about finding The One? First and foremost you must be patient. Don't rush into anything. It's ok to wait and take your time and get to know YOU. Ah-uh, you thought I was going to say 'get to know them'. When I know who I am, what I like, what I don't like, what my hang ups are what I'm willing to put up with and what I'm not willing to put up with then I can recognize my true counterpart when presented. Just like Adam recognized Eve. Second, and this is crucial, you must trust in the Lord and wait on His timing and follow His lead. Going ahead of God will only get you in trouble and linger behind God will only get you delayed. We must allow God into our lives NOW! And let Him direct our steps straight into the path of **"The One."**

ABOUT THE AUTHOR

Elder Cloretta Denean Chandler is known as a singer, preacher, teacher, mentor, author and entrepreneur but the truth is she's a down to earth kind a woman who loves God and cares for people.

Cloretta is a native of Pueblo, Colorado, the youngest of four siblings raised in a family of faith in God through Christ Jesus. As a P.K. (preacher's kid) Cloretta learned the value and worth of being a child of God. She was afforded the opportunity to learn the integral workings of a viable and successful ministry. These lessons have become a fundamental part of her life.

In 1998 she accepted her call into the ministry and was licensed in 1999. From the time she was licensed Cloretta developed into a powerful prognosticator of the gospel and has been described as "A Quiet Storm" whose delivery and presentation of the Word draws you in and explodes with wisdom and revelation. In 2004 Cloretta received here Certificate of Ordination and is currently pursuing a Master' degree in Divinity.

Cloretta's belief and message is that "in order to reach our full potential in Christ we must know who we are as children of God. We must come to the to realize that because of Christ we are no longer bound by the guilt of our past, by sin or shame. We have been given a kingdom inheritance full of power to overcome every obstacle, every heart ache and every pain."

www.ingramcontent.com/pod-product-compliance
Lightning Source LLC
Chambersburg PA
CBHW061515040426
42450CB00008B/1637